Fact Finders®

ENDANGERED RIVERS

INVESTIGATING RIVERS IN CRISIS

by Rani Iyer

Content Consultant:
Thomas M. Neeson, PhD
Postdoctoral Researcher
Department of Limnology
University of Wisconsin—Madison

CAPSTONE PRESS
a capstone imprint

Fact Finders Books are published by Capstone Press,
1710 Roe Crest Drive, North Mankato, Minnesota 56003
www.capstonepub.com

Library of Congress Cataloging-in-Publication Data
Cataloging-in-Publication Data is on file with the Library of Congress.

ISBN: 978-1-4914-2040-9 (library binding)
ISBN: 978-1-4914-2215-1 (paperback)
ISBN: 978-1-4914-2230-4 (eBook PDF)

Editorial Credits
Abby Colich, editor; Bobbie Nuytten, designer; Gina Kammer, media researcher;
Tori Abraham, production specialist

Photo Credits
Corbis: © Bettmann, 13, © Bob Sacha, 17, © John Gress, 22, JAI/© Jane Sweeney, 27; Dreamstime:
Mikhail Blajenov (top), 23; Getty Images: Dorling Kindersley, 6; Newscom: EPA/KHALED EL-FIQI, 21,
Ingram Publishing, (bottom), 23, REUTERS/BRAZIL/STRINGER, 20, REUTERS/NIR ELIAS, 25; North
Wind Picture Archives: 8; Shutterstock: alexmisu (top left), cover, Arseniy Krasnevsky (back), cover, 1,
Asianet-Pakistan, 9, Baloncici, 18, Colin Stitt (top right), cover, cubephoto, 24, Geoffrey Kuchera, 29,
guentermanaus, 5, irisphoto1, 19, joppo, 12, Kekyalyaynen, 26, KPG Ivary, 28, Luciano Queiroz, 7,
niall dunne, 4, Oliver Sved (bottom left), cover, Sasilssolutions, 14, Strahil Dimitrov, 15, Vadym Zaitsev,
16, wk1003mike, 10, WvdM (bottom right), cover, Zorandim, 11

Printed in Canada.
092014   008478FRS15

Table of Contents

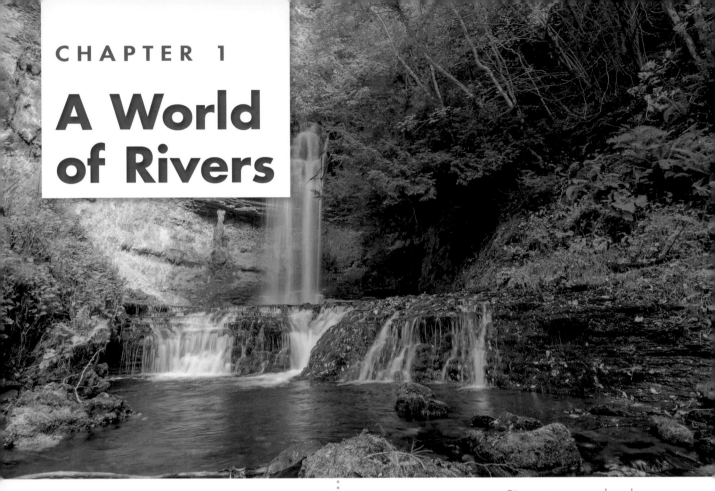

CHAPTER 1
A World of Rivers

Rivers, streams, and creeks flow on every continent on Earth.

Water rushes over rocks and down a waterfall. Beavers build dams with tree branches. A bird swoops down and grabs a fish with its bill. Crayfish munch on algae. All sorts of creatures live in or near rivers. People depend on rivers for survival too. In the United States, 65 percent of drinking water comes from rivers and streams. Rivers are an important part of Earth's landscape.

As much as humans rely on rivers, they have caused much harm to this resource. Human actions have **endangered** rivers. Several rivers are running dry. Others are severely **polluted**. Some fish **species** that once thrived are now nearly **extinct**. Experts believe that the world will suffer a major water crisis if rivers are not cleaned up and protected.

endanger—to put at risk

pollute—to make something dirty or unsafe

species—a group of plants or animals that share common characteristics

extinct—no longer living; an extinct species is one that has died out, with no more of its kind

Rivers around the world are becoming littered with trash.

Parts of a River

source — the place where a river begins, usually a spring, glacier, or lake

tributary — a creek, stream, brook, or other river that flows into a larger river

channel — the course a river takes through land

meander — a bend or turn in a river's channel

bank — the land alongside a river

floodplain — area of land next to a river where water can overflow

delta — area of land that forms at the mouth of a river

mouth — where a river ends, usually into another river or the sea

What Is a River?

A river is a body of freshwater. Its **current** flows in one direction. Rivers usually start in high places. They flow downhill and empty into another body of water.

No two rivers are alike. The shape and course of a river changes over time. Some rivers, such as the Rhine in Europe, are deep and wide and flow slowly. Other rivers, such as the Trinity River in California, rush quickly, creating rapids and waterfalls. Some rivers flow only during seasons of heavy rain. Occasionally some rivers flow partly underground.

Life in a River

current — the movement of water in a river or an ocean

ecosystem — a group of animals and plants that interact with their surroundings

invertebrate — an animal without a backbone

food web — many food chains connected to one another

Rivers and the organisms they support form a complex **ecosystem**. A perfect place for life to thrive, rivers are home to almost every kind of organism. Trees and other plants grow in the river and along its banks. Insects and other **invertebrates** float on the surface and crawl on the riverbed below. Rivers are filled with fish. Frogs, turtles, snakes, and otters also call rivers home. Life too small to see, such as phytoplankton, is an important part of river **food webs**.

Fish are just one of many organisms in a river's ecosystem.

7

Rivers and People

People have settled near rivers throughout history. Ancient peoples built cities along riverbanks. They used river water to grow crops. They fished and built boats to travel. They traveled down rivers to trade for goods.

People continue to use rivers in the same way today. Rivers provide water that is used for drinking, bathing, cooking, and cleaning. Freshwater fish are an important part of the diets of millions of people. Ferries carry people over rivers from one place to another. Millions of tons of goods travel down rivers every day.

..... Fur traders load a canoe on the Bear River in Utah.

Humans have newer uses for rivers too. River water can generate **hydroelectric** power. Some kinds of fish and shrimp are farmed in rivers. Rivers support sports and recreational activities.

The water in the air, rivers, lakes, and underground stores accounts for 1 percent of all water on Earth. This 1 percent must provide freshwater for everyone on Earth. The rest of Earth's water is in the oceans and frozen in polar ice caps.

.... life on the Indus River in Sukkur, Pakistan

CHAPTER 2

Pollution and Rivers

From drinking water to food, rivers provide for many human needs. But humans have also severely damaged rivers. Scientists say half of the world's major rivers are seriously polluted. Pollution comes from many different places. It can come from farms, industries, and people. It is a constant threat to life within rivers.

Pollution from Farming

Farming is the leading cause of pollution in many areas today. Most farmers choose to use fertilizers and pesticides to help grow their crops. Many fertilizers and pesticides contain chemicals that are toxic. When crops are watered or rain falls, the chemicals wash off with the water. The **runoff** flows into nearby rivers.

Large numbers of dead fish are now appearing more frequently in rivers due to pollution.

These chemicals damage rivers in many ways. The chemicals from fertilizers help plants grow. But in a river they can cause extra algae to grow. When the algae dies, it takes oxygen away from other organisms. The chemicals in pesticides kill pests that harm crops. If they end up in a river, they can kill fish, birds, and other creatures.

In addition to chemicals, animal waste also flows from farms into rivers. This causes a loss in the amount of oxygen in a river. Animals that live in the river can die as a result.

runoff—water that flows over land instead of soaking into the ground

This farmer is treating his wheat crop with a chemical pesticide.

Industrial Pollution

Industrial pollution is any waste that comes from an industry or business. Since the 19th century, factories that make items such as clothing, paper, and medicine have dumped their liquid waste into rivers. This waste contains substances that are toxic. Sometimes these toxins kill fish and other animals right away. Other times they enter the **food chain** when small fish eat plants. Bigger fish build up toxins in their bodies when they eat smaller fish. These bigger fish can in turn be toxic to humans who eat them. Other times companies dump liquid waste into rivers that is much hotter than the water temperature. River life that cannot handle the rise in temperature is threatened.

food chain — series of organisms in which each one in the series eats the one preceding it

industrial waste flowing into a river

Cuyahoga River Fire

An incident several decades ago led to major improvements for U.S. rivers. In 1969 pollution caused part of the Cuyahoga River in Ohio to catch on fire. The fire was small, but people were angered. This was not the first time the river had caught on fire. The first fire was in 1936. The river caught fire several more times, including a very large fire in 1952. But the response to the 1969 fire led to the creation of new laws in 1972. These laws put limits on what companies could dump into water.

Over the last decades, governments have passed laws that have helped reduce the amount of waste companies can dump into water. But that doesn't stop some companies from illegally dumping their waste. The laws are not easy to enforce. In some places there are no laws that prevent this pollution. Industrial waste remains a threat to the world's rivers.

...Cuyahoga River fire of 1952

Sewage

Where does the water from toilets, bathtubs, and sinks go? Human waste, soaps, cleaners, and everything else that goes down the drain often ends up in rivers. In some areas sewage is cleaned in a treatment plant. The treated water is then dumped into rivers. But not all toxins can be removed during treatment. Many harmful pollutants still enter the water. Over time these can poison life that depends on the river water, including humans. There are many areas all over the world where sewage is not treated or cleaned before it is dumped into rivers. People who swim or bathe in the water can become ill. Wildlife is poisoned.

sewage drain releasing dirty water

... trash illegally dumped near a river

Litter and Dumping

Litter, or any kind of solid trash, might be the most obvious kind of river pollution. Some people carelessly throw trash in rivers. Other times litter is carried by wind or storm drains. The trash dirties the water. It also harms river life. Fish or birds swallow bits of trash that they think is food. This damages the animals' bodies and sometimes kills them. Other times they are caught or tangled in trash and become trapped. When litter such as plastic breaks down, it releases toxins that poison the water. These toxins are harmful to the life that depends on the water.

From Air to Water

Pollution from the air also harms rivers. Carbon dioxide is a gas that occurs naturally in the air. This gas is also released into the air when people use certain fuels such as gasoline. Over time too much carbon dioxide has collected in the air. Carbon dioxide naturally helps trap heat on Earth. But too much carbon dioxide is causing Earth to become warmer. If the Earth becomes too warm, the environment is at risk.

Pollutants in the air also affect rivers.

Warmer temperatures are causing some rivers to dry up. In some areas, changes in climate are causing less **precipitation**. Less rain and snow means less water for rivers. Also, when water warms, it **evaporates** more quickly, causing rivers to dry up. River life cannot thrive without enough water.

While some rivers are drying up, others are flooding more often. Warmer temperatures cause snow and ice to melt. Some areas are receiving more rain and snow than what is normal. These factors lead to more flooding. It is normal for rivers to flood sometimes. But an increase of flooding is harmful to rivers and the humans who live near them. When floodwater **recedes**, oil, gas, chemicals from farms, and trash go with it. The water fills with toxins that are harmful to life in and near the water.

precipitation—falling of water from the sky in the form of rain, sleet, hail, or snow

evaporate—to change from liquid into gas

recede—to move back and away

.... This river in Xun County, China, is nearly dried up.

17

CHAPTER 3

More Damage

Flooding has destroyed this roadway.

Pollution is not the only thing harming the world's rivers. Development, fishing, overuse, and **invasive species** all play a part in harming river water and the life that depends on it.

Development along Rivers

Throughout history, people have settled near rivers. But over time, people began building bigger structures closer to rivers. This causes pollution to more easily enter rivers. Many times floodplain areas are developed. When rivers flood, the water has nowhere else to go. Water fills the floodplain. When water recedes, pollution and litter travels with it.

Parts of a Dam

reservoir

dam wall

powerhouse

outflow

Dams

Dams are structures built to stop the flow of river water. The water is collected and held in a reservoir. Dams have many benefits. They supply water for crops, create hydroelectric power, and provide drinking water. But dams disrupt the natural flow of rivers. When dams block their environment, fish cannot move to **breed** or find food. Dams also trap **sediment**. Areas downstream need sediment. Lack of sediment causes erosion. Too much **erosion** can kill plants and trees that grow along a riverbank.

invasive species—plants or animals that have been artificially introduced into an ecosystem

breed—to mate and produce young

sediment—bits of sand or clay carried by water or wind

erosion—the wearing away of land by water or wind

Overfishing

In many countries people rely on freshwater fish as a main source of protein. Without limits on the amount fishers can catch, the number of fish has declined. When one species runs low, fishers begin catching another. If this trend continues, scientists believe the world's rivers will reach dangerously low levels of fish. Several species of river fish are now endangered due to overfishing. These include the arapaima in the Amazon River and Murray cod in Australia. The sockeye salmon is endangered in some rivers in the United States.

... Fishing of the arapaima is now allowed only once a year in Brazil.

.... fish farm in the Nile River in Egypt

Overuse

People have always depended on rivers for their survival. As the human population has grown, so has the impact on rivers. Rivers are used for farming, industry, and drinking water. Experts say if this pressure on rivers continues, some rivers may dry up before they reach the sea. One place where this is particularly true is China. Parts of the Yellow River have dried up due to overuse.

People must find ways to reduce the amount of water used from rivers. Continued overuse of river water will impact people and wildlife in many negative ways.

Fish Farms

Pollution is killing many fish. Too much fishing is also leading to a decline in the number of wild fish. People are now creating fish farms in some rivers. Fish farms can help increase food supplies. Cages of carp, tilapia, salmon, and catfish are raised on farms in some rivers. But fish farms can harm rivers. Food for the fish can cause the growth of too much algae. Also, when so many fish live too close together, they can become diseased. Diseases can spread to other life in the river, including wild fish.

Invasive Species

Invasive species are plants and animals that move from their habitat into a new one. Sometimes they arrive in a new habitat accidentally. They may be carried by boat. Sometimes humans introduce them to a new area on purpose. Invasive species multiply and eventually harm a local ecosystem. Some invasive species prey on local species. Other invasive species take resources and habitat away from local species. Local species can decline to the point of becoming endangered. Invasive species many times have no predators in their new environment. They continue to reproduce and take over the new area.

In the United States, some species of Asian carp were introduced in some rivers. People wanted the carp to help control algae growth. But the carp quickly spread. They feed on snails and mussels, some of which are now endangered. The carp now threaten several ecosystems in lakes and rivers.

Asian carp

River Life at Risk

All over the world, river life is affected by the harm humans have caused to rivers. Many river species are now endangered.

The Mekong catfish is found in Asia's Mekong River. This giant catfish weighs about 660 pounds (300 kilograms). Overfishing and damming have led to this fish's decline.

The river terrapin was once abundant in parts of Asia. But this turtle, along with its eggs, are hunted for food.

The population of the Southern River Otter, native to South America, has declined in recent years. Habitat destruction and illegal hunting are to blame.

The green pitcher plant was once common along rivers in the Southeastern United States. There are only a handful of these insect-eating plants remaining in the wild. Development as well as collection for commercial trade have led to its decline.

An environmental researcher takes samples from a river.

CHAPTER 4

Saving the Rivers

The world's rivers are drying up, flooding more often, and full of pollution. Some species are declining. Ecosystems are changing. But people still depend on rivers for survival. This vital resource must be cleaned up and protected. What needs to happen to save the world's rivers?

Better Laws

In the United States, the Clean Water Act of 1972 continues to have a major impact on the country's rivers. The amount of industrial pollution dumped into rivers has drastically decreased. But nearly half of all freshwater in the United States is considered to be unhealthy. More laws are needed to stop pollution from farms and other sources.

Drinking Water
from the Sea

Some areas are turning to oceans for their drinking water as rivers dry up. Factories that take salt out of seawater are now found throughout the world. After the salt is removed, the water is supplied to cities. However, the process requires a lot of energy. Using this extra energy releases more carbon dioxide into the air.

More laws to protect freshwater are needed around the world too. Many rivers run through more than one country. Polluted water from one country flows into another. The United Nations is one organization working to protect the world's water. It launched the "Water for Life" decade in 2005. Countries must work together to create laws to protect the world's water.

•••••• desalinization plant on the Mediterranean Sea in Hadera, Israel

Slow Down Development

Many people live along riverbanks. Some businesses prosper near rivers. People depend on dams for many uses. Governments are removing some dams to improve the health of rivers. But it's not practical to tear down all development near rivers. People and governments must work together to stop more development along rivers. Less development will prevent further pollution and protect river life.

Better Farming

If land can be better protected from pollution, then rivers will benefit too. Less toxic pesticides and fertilizers must be developed and used. Ways to prevent toxic runoff must also be developed. If the world changes the way it farms, a leading cause of river pollution will end.

Better Sewage Treatment

Pollution from sewage is a problem for many rivers. Even sewage that has been treated and cleaned can still poison river life. Scientists must work to develop better water treatment systems. People must be educated about what is safe to flush down the toilet. Governments must make the necessary updates to sewage systems.

These storage tanks prevent waste water from being released into a river.

River Success

With careful planning, it is possible to improve the condition of some rivers. In the 1950s a highway was built on top of the Cheonggyecheon, a stream in Seoul, South Korea. A project to restore the 7-mile (11-kilometer) long stream was launched in 2003. Officials decided to tear down the highway and let the water flow free again. Native trees were planted along the riverbanks. Soon fish, birds, and animals began returning to the water.

Better Energy

Some people are pushing the world to use cleaner energy. This energy produces little or no carbon dioxide. Less extra carbon dioxide in the air will help prevent higher temperatures on Earth. This will slow climate change and its negative effects on rivers.

the Cheonggyecheon stream in Seoul, South Korea

People Doing Their Part

It will take a global effort to clean up the world's rivers. But everyone can make changes at home that will help keep rivers clean.

Conserve water.

Make sure that washing machines and dishwashers are full before starting. Turn off the sink when brushing teeth. Take shorter showers. Taking a short shower instead of filling up a bathtub can save 11 gallons (42 liters) of water.

Be mindful of what is flushed.

Water treatment plants can't remove everything. By not flushing harmful substances such as medicine down the toilet, river life can be spared from being exposed to some toxins.

Use less electricity and fuels.

When fossil fuels are used, carbon dioxide is released into the air. The more carbon dioxide in the air, the warmer the Earth is going to get. More damage to the planet, including rivers, is going to occur.

Volunteer with a local river or stream clean up program.

Plant native tree species near riverbanks. Tree roots hold soil in place and help control floodwaters during the rainy seasons.

Keep water clean.

Throw trash away in its proper place. Don't litter. It may end up in a river. Don't dump anything down a storm drain. Anything dumped likely ends up in a river.

A lot of change must happen. There's a lot of work to do to clean up the world's rivers. The people of the world must work together prevent more damage. But rivers are a resource definitely worth saving and protecting.

Glossary

breed (BREED)—to mate and produce young

current (KUHR-uhnt)—the movement of water in a river or an ocean

ecosystem (EE-koh-sis-tuhm)—a group of animals and plants that interact with their surroundings

endanger (in-DAYN-juhr)—to put at risk

erosion (i-ROH-zhuhn)—the wearing away of land by water or wind

evaporate (i-VA-puh-rayt)—to change from liquid into gas

extinct (ik-STINGKT)—no longer living; an extinct species is one that has died out, with no more of its kind

food chain (FEWD CHAIN)—series of organisms in which each one in the series eats the one preceding it

food web (FEWD WEB)—many food chains connected to one another

hydroelectric (hye-droh-i-LEK-trik)—to do with the production of electricity from moving water

invasive species (in-VAY-siv SPEE-sheez)—plants or animals that have been artificially introduced into an ecosystem

invertebrate (in-VUR-tuh-bruht)—an animal without a backbone

pollute (puh-LOOT)—to make something dirty or unsafe

precipitation (pri-sip-i-TAY-shuhn)—falling of water from the sky in the form of rain, sleet, hail, or snow

recede (ri-SEED)—to move back and away

runoff (ruhn-AWF)—water that flows over land instead of soaking into the ground

sediment (SED-uh-muhnt)—bits of sand or clay carried by water or wind

species (SPEE-sheez)—a group of plants or animals that share common characteristics

Critical Thinking Using the Common Core

1. How have humans damaged the world's rivers? Use evidence from the text to support your answers. (Key Idea and Details)

2. Look at the photos on pages 8 and 9. Based on what you've read in the text, how do you think human interactions with rivers have changed over time? How have they stayed the same? (Craft and Structure)

3. How might the world be different if clean and renewable energy sources were more commonly used than fossil fuels. Use evidence from the text and other print and reliable Internet sources to support your answer. (Integration of Knowledge and Ideas)

Read More

Goodman, Polly. *Rivers in Danger*. Earth Alert! New York: Gareth Stevens, 2012.

Kaye, Cathryn Berger. *Make a Splash! A Kid's Guide to Protecting Our Oceans, Lakes, Rivers, and Wetlands*. Minneapolis: Free Spirit, 2013.

Waldron, Melanie. *Rivers*. Habitat Survival. Chicago: Raintree, 2013.

Internet Sites

FactHound offers a safe, fun way to find Internet sites related to this book. All of the sites on FactHound have been researched by our staff.

Here's all you do:

Visit *www.facthound.com*

Type in this code: 9781491420409

Check out projects, games and lots more at
www.capstonekids.com

Index